MEXICAN COOKING

TARLA DALAL

S&C

SANJAY & CO.
BOMBAY

Ninth Printing : 2006

ISBN : 81-86469-10-9

Price Rs. 189/-

Published & Distributed by :
Sanjay & Company
353/A-1, Shah & Nahar Industrial Estate, Dhanraj Mill Compound,
Lower Parel (W), Mumbai - 400 013. INDIA.
Tel. : (91-22) 2496 8068 • Fax : (91-22) 2496 5876 • E-mail : sanjay@tarladalal.com
Printed by : **Minal Sales Agencies**, Mumbai

: Designed by :	: Food Stylist :
Mr. Niranjan Kamatkar	Nitin Tandon
: Photography :	: Production Designers :
Vinay Mahidar	Lorella Jacinto
	Preeti Braganza

OTHER BOOKS BY TARLA DALAL

INDIAN COOKING
Tava Cooking
Rotis & Subzis
Desi Khana
The Complete Gujarati Cook Book
Mithai
Chaat
Achaar aur Parathe
The Rajasthani Cookbook
Swadisht Subzian

WESTERN COOKING
The Complete Italian Cookbook
The Chocolate Cookbook
Eggless Desserts
Mocktails & Snacks
Soups & Salads
Easy Gourmet Cooking
Chinese Cooking
Easy Chinese Cooking
Thai Cooking
Sizzlers & Barbeques

TOTAL HEALTH
Low Calorie Healthy Cooking
Pregnancy Cookbook
Baby and Toddler Cookbook
Cooking with 1 Teaspoon of Oil
Home Remedies
Delicious Diabetic Recipes
Fast Foods Made Healthy
Healthy Soups & Salads
Healthy Breakfast

MINI SERIES
A new world of Idlis & Dosas
Cooking under 10 minutes
Pizzas and Pastas
Fun Food for Kids
Roz Ka Khana
Microwave - Desi Khana
T.V. Meals
Paneer
Parathas
Chawal

GENERAL COOKING
Exciting Vegetarian Cooking
Party Cooking
Microwave Cooking
Quick & Easy Cooking
Saatvik Khana
Mixer Cook Book

The Pleasures of Vegetarian Cooking
The Delights of Vegetarian Cooking
The Joys of Vegetarian Cooking
Cooking With Kids
Snacks Under 10 Minutes
Ice-Cream & Frozen Desserts
Desserts Under 10 Minutes

MEXICAN COOKING

INDEX

MAIN DISHES

DESSERTS

BASIC RECIPES

INTRODUCTION

Mexican cuisine is not only colourful and tangy but immensely varied. Yet for some strange reasons many people seem to think of it as Nachos and Tacos. Nothing could be further from the truth, as this book will show you.

Mexicans love to eat; those who can afford to manage to eat four meals a day. Breakfast starts the day. In the cities, this tends to be light, consisting of sweet rolls and coffee or hot chocolate. At midday, most Mexicans have their main meal, or *comida*. This meal , a two hour affair, is the centre of daily life for Mexicans. For it, the husband comes home from work; the children, from school. After the meal, there is usually a siesta, a virtual necessity after so many courses. Later, at around six in the afternoon, it is time for *merienda*, a small meal similar to the English teatime. The Mexicans drink coffee or hot chocolate and eat cakes and cookies and pastries. Then, sometime between eight and 10 in the evening, there is supper. For those who have made the comida their big meal, supper or cena, will be light.

The presentation of food is quite important. The Mexicans are the most fanciful craftsmen in the world. Their brightly coloured pottery plates are decorated with birds and animals, their intricate silver dishes, their exquisite table-cloths, their woven mats and their hand-blown glasses and even their great primitive earthenware jugs and casseroles are all a delight to the eye. The presence of such articles on a Mexican table makes the entire meal immediately inviting and exciting.

Mexican drinks, such as tequila and the wine punch sangria, have become immensely and justifiably popular. Tequila is made from the sap in the starchy roots of the agave plant, a succulent which also provides fiber for twine, mats, and clothing. It is normally colourless, although some types of tequila are aged in a way that gives them a pale yellow colour. While it has a reputation for being very potent, it is actually no stronger than whiskey. It can be drunk straight or made into a delicious cocktail called a Margarita in which lime juice, sugar and a dash of Cointreau or triple sec are added to the tequila. Because tequila and salt go together beautifully (Mexicans often drink their straight tequilla by putting a pinch of salt on the back of one hand, tossing the salt into their mouth downing the tequila with the other hand), Margaritas are served in cold glasses that have been dipped into coarse salt so that the salt forms a crystal frosting around the glass edge.

Mexican cuisine begins with tortillas. Tortilla is the bread of Mexico. Both corn and flour tortillas are frequently served as bread in a soft, steamy-hot form (often folded and wrapped in a napkin which helps keep them warm as long as possible). Tortillas should be present at any Mexican meals and form the basis of some of the more famous Mexican dishes, such as tostadas, burritos, quesadillas, tacos, enchiladas and nachos.

Tostadas : A tostada is a crisp fried tortilla that makes the bottom layer and then beans and cheese are piled high. The ingredients traditionally offer contrasts of soft and crisp, hot and cold, sharp and mild. While the Mexicans put meat in the tostadas, we have used cottage cheese.

Burritos : A burrito consists of a soft flour tortilla to enclose a filling such as refried beans with cheese.

Quesadillas : A quesadilla contains a cheese filling to which seasoning such as green chillies may be added; the tortilla may be open flat with cheese melted on top or folded over with cheese.

Tacos : Half moon shaped tacos are probably the most popular Mexican food in America. The word "taco" means "snack" and is generally referred to as a crisp fried corn tortilla folded in half to form a pocket which is filled with a stuffing, garnish and spicy sauce.

Enchiladas : Enchiladas are tortillas which are rolled around a filling.

Nachos : Cheese is melted over corn chips and heated quickly in the oven to make nachos. Guests pull out individual chips to eat with their fingers.

Beans appear at every Mexican meal, and a bubbling pot of beans is omnipresent in the Mexican kitchen. Served as a starchy accompaniment, they are mashed as refried beans and offered as a filling or topping for other dishes.

Another food that is typically Mexican and which is served in many intriguing ways in Mexico is the avocado. This fruit grows so profusely in tropical climates that even poor Mexican families can enjoy this delicious fruit frequently. The most popular way of preparing avocado is to mash the insides with tomatoes and spices, making the famous guacamole.

No account of Mexican cuisine would be complete without mentioning chiles. All peppers are called chiles in Mexico, whether they are sweet and green or red and fiery hot. There are over ninety different varieties of chiles in Mexico. I have given the recipes for jalapenos, pasilla chiles, serrano chiles and crushed red pepper, which are made from local ingredients easily available. I have similarly modified many recipes to adjust to locally available ingredients.

It is highly advisable for the beginner to study the basic recipes and then proceed through the book. All the recipes in this book are simple to follow and are explained step by step. Through extensive research, I have provided you with a wide variety of vegetarian Mexican recipes which I am sure you will enjoy making.

COCONUT AND PAPAYA DRINK

picture on page 35

◀ *A very nourishing drink, with the lovely flavour of coconut.*

Preparation time : a few minutes.   **No cooking.**   **Makes 6 small glasses.**

$1/2$ coconut
4 cups melon or papaya pieces
sugar to taste (around 3 teaspoons per glass)
crushed ice

1. Grate the coconut. Add 1 cup of water and blend in a liquidiser. Strain and take out the coconut milk. Keep aside.

2. Mix the coconut milk, melon, sugar and crushed ice.

3. Blend in a blender. Strain.

Serve cold.

MARGARITA

◀ *If you make freshly squeezed lime margaritas, you will make a name for yourself. There is no substitute for the aromatic fresh lime and, believe me, the satisfaction of making the most delicious margarita in town is enough reward for the hard work of squeezing the limes!*

◀ *If you are having a party and you need several margaritas, squeeze all the limes together, mix with the measured tequila and Triple Sec or Cointreau, and refrigerate. Prepare the rims of the glasses as instructed and have them ready to pour the margarita mixture over the crushed ice as your guests arrive.*

Preparation time : 5 minutes.   No cooking.   Serves 4.

225 ml. tequila
4 tablespoons Triple Sec or Cointreau
2 large limes
8 ice cubes
table salt

1.   Squeeze the juice from the limes, reserving the lime halves. Moisten the rims of four cocktail glasses by rubbing with the reserved squeezed lime halves. Put the salt on a saucer and dip the rim of the glasses in it. (Do not attempt to do this with water as it dissolves the salt).

2.   Place the lime juice in a blender, add the tequila, the Triple Sec or Cointreau and the ice cubes, and blend at high speed for 30 seconds. Pour into the chilled glasses. If you wish to make this drink weaker, add more ice and less of the mixture to each glass.

FRUIT DAIQUIRI

Preparation time : 10 minutes.   No cooking.   Makes 1 glass.

1 teacup cut fruit (strawberries, black grapes, pineapple, bananas etc.)
2 tablespoons sugar syrup
2 teaspoons lemon juice
1 teacup crushed ice
60 ml. white rum

For decoration
pineapple slices

1.   Put in a liquidiser the cut fruit, sugar syrup, lemon juice, white rum and crushed ice.

2.   Blend for 1 minute. Pour into a tall glass.

Decorate with pineapple slices and serve cold.

CLEAR GAZPACHO

picture on page 18

◀ *A chilled Mexican soup, ideal for the summer.*

Preparation time : 10 minutes. Cooking time : 10 minutes. Makes 6 cups.

For the stock
1 cucumber
1 onion

Other ingredients
2 tomatoes, chopped

For the topping
1 tablespoon salad oil
1 teaspoon sugar
1 tablespoon chopped coriander
1 chopped tomato
1 tablespoon chopped capsicum
1 tablespoon chopped cucumber
a few drops of Tabasco sauce
salt to taste

1. Cut the cucumber and onion into big pieces. Add 6 cups of water and cook.

2. When cooked, add the tomatoes and blend in a blender. Pass through a sieve.

3. Put the topping in the soup, add a few ice cubes and mix well.

Serve cold.

KIDNEY BEAN (RAJMA) SOUP

◀ *This piquant soup is ideal for the winter.*

Preparation time : 10 minutes. Cooking time : 15 minutes. Serves 6.

1 cup red kidney beans (rajma)
2 onions, chopped
4 tomatoes, chopped
3 cloves garlic
$1/_2$ teaspoon chilli powder
1 teaspoon lemon juice
2 tablespoons oil
salt to taste

For serving
finely chopped tomatoes
sliced green onions
chopped coriander
Tabasco sauce

1. Wash the beans and soak in water overnight. Next day, drain. Wash thoroughly.

2. Heat the oil, add the onions and fry for 1 minute. Add the tomatoes, garlic, chilli powder and salt and fry again for 1 minute.

3. Add the beans and 6 cups of water and cook in a pressure cooker. Blend in a blender. Do not strain.

4. Add the lemon juice.

Serve hot with tomatoes, onions, coriander and Tabasco sauce.

TORTILLA SOUP

◄ *A tasty tomato based soup which is topped with corn chips, sour cream and cheese.*

Preparation time : 20 minutes. Cooking time : 30 minutes. Serves 6.

1 kg. ripe tomatoes, chopped
3 teaspoons cornflour
2 cups corn chips, page 26
100 grams cottage cheese (paneer), chopped
2 tablespoons cooked corn kernels
1 onion, chopped
$1/2$ seasoning cube, vegetarian
$1/2$ teaspoon sugar
2 tablespoons butter
salt to taste

For the garnish
fresh cream
grated cheese

1. Add 5 cups of water to the tomatoes and cook. Blend in a blender and pass through a sieve.

2. Heat the butter and fry the onion for 1/2 minute.

3. Mix the cornflour in 1 cup of water.

4. Add the tomato mixture and cornflour mixture to the onion and bring to a boil.

5. Add the cottage cheese, corn, seasoning cube, sugar and salt and cook for a few minutes.

6. Just before serving, add the corn chips and top with cream and grated cheese.

Serve hot.

SOPA DE MILHO VERDE (GREEN CORN SOUP)

◄ *Mexicans have used their popular 'corn' to make a mild corn soup flavoured with green onions.*

Preparation time : 10 minutes. Cooking time : 10 minutes. Serves 6.

3 cups cooked sweet corn
$1^1/_2$ cups milk
1 cup chopped green onions
2 tablespoons plain flour (maida)
2 tablespoons butter
salt and pepper to taste

1. Put the corn, milk and green onions in a mixer and blend into a smooth pur´ee.

2. Heat the butter and fry the flour for $^1/_2$ minute.

3. Add the corn mixture, 2 cups of water and salt and pepper and cook for 4 to 5 minutes.

Serve hot.

SOPA DE CHICHARO (GREEN PEA SOUP)

◄ *Green peas are cooked, puréed and then mixed with corn to give a delightfully mild flavoured soup.*

Preparation time : 15 minutes. Cooking time : 15 minutes. Serves 4.

2 cups fresh green peas
$^1/_2$ onion, chopped
1 clove garlic, crushed
1 tablespoon plain flour (maida)
$^1/_4$ teaspoon chilli powder
1 cup cooked sweet corn kernels, crushed
1 tablespoon butter
1 teaspoon salt

For serving
fresh cream
chopped coriander
grated cheese
chopped parsley

1. Mix the peas, onion, garlic and 4 cups of water and boil for 10 minutes until tender. Blend in a mixer and strain.

2. Heat the butter, add the flour and cook for 1 minute.

3. Add the peas mixture, chilli powder, corn and salt and cook for 2 minutes.

4. When you want to serve, add the cream, coriander, parsley and cheese.

Serve hot.

SWEET CORN AND CAPSICUM SOUP

◀ *A typical Mexican smoky flavoured capsicum and sweet corn soup. Remember sweet corn is yellow in colour and can almost be eaten raw.*

Preparation time : 15 minutes. Cooking time : 10 minutes. Serves 6.

$1/2$ cup milk
$1^1/_2$ cups cooked sweet corn kernels
$1/2$ onion, chopped
1 capsicum
1 tablespoon cornflour
1 tablespoon butter
salt to taste

1. Pierce the capsicum with a fork and hold over the flame until the skin blackens. Remove from the heat, rub off the burnt skin and chop.
2. Heat the butter and fry the onion for $1/2$ minute.
3. Add the capsicum and fry again for a while.
4. Blend the milk, corn and 3 cups of water in a blender. Add to the onion-capsicum mixture.
5. Mix the cornflour with 1 cup of water and add to the soup.
6. Add salt and boil for 4 to 5 minutes.

Serve hot.

MEXICAN MINESTRONE

◀ *Mexicans have adapted the Italian Minestrone with corn and mushrooms to suit their palates.*

Preparation time : 15 minutes. Cooking time : 15 minutes. Makes 6 cups.

$^1/_2$ cup cucumber, finely chopped
6 cups brown stock, page 78
1 cup cooked corn kernels
2 tablespoons sliced mushrooms
2 tablespoons chopped onions
2 large tomatoes, peeled and chopped
1 tablespoon chopped coriander
1 cup chopped spinach
1 tablespoon butter
salt to taste

For serving
2 tablespoons grated cheese

1. Put the tomatoes in hot water for 10 minutes. Take out the skin and chop them.

2. Heat the butter and fry the onions for a few seconds.

3. Add the corn, mushrooms and salt and cook for 2 to 3 minutes.

4. Add the tomatoes, spinach, cucumber and brown stock and boil.

Serve hot garnished with the coriander and cheese.

BLACK BEAN SOUP

picture on page 35

◀ *A traditional mildly flavoured Mexican soup.*

Preparation time : 10 minutes. Cooking time : 15 minutes. Serves 6.

1 cup black beans
4 large tomatoes
1 onion, chopped
2 cloves garlic, crushed
2 tablespoons butter
salt to taste

For serving
toast pieces

1. Soak the black beans for 6 hours. Add 5 cups of water and the tomatoes and garlic. Cook in a pressure cooker and then blend in a mixer. Do not strain the mixture.

2. Heat the butter and fry the onion for $1/2$ minute.

3. Add the soup and salt and cook for a few minutes.

4. Top with toast pieces.

Serve hot.

Mexican ingredients : Garlic, White onions, Serrano chillies, Jalapeno chillies, ▶
Red capsicum, Lettuce, Yellow capsicum, Corn, Zucchini, Iceburg lettuce,
Baby tomatoes, Red cabbage, Halapeno chillies, Kashmiri chillies, Black beans,
Haricot beans, Kidney beans.

ENSALADA DE EJOTES (GREEN BEAN SALAD)

◄ *Green beans taste great when topped with vinegar dressing and served cold.*

Preparation time : 10 minutes. Cooking time : 10 minutes. Serves 6.

2 cups tender french beans, diagonally cut
1 cup sliced baby corn
1 cup sliced tomatoes
3 tablespoons capsicum, sliced

To be mixed into a dressing (in a bottle)
$1/3$ cup olive oil or cooking oil
2 tablespoons vinegar
1 tablespoon lemon juice
1 tablespoon parsley or coriander, chopped
2 teaspoons sugar
2 pinches black pepper
$1/2$ teaspoon oregano
salt to taste

1. Blanch the baby corn in salted water.

2. Boil the french beans in salted water.

3. Pour the dressing over the french beans, baby corn, capsicum and tomatoes. Cover and place in the refrigerator.

Serve cold on a bed of lettuce.

◄ Top : Burnt Corn Salad, page 23 ; Bottom : Gazpacho, page 9.

KIDNEY BEAN SALAD

◀ *A tasty and nutritious accompaniment for barbeque parties.*

Preparation time : 10 minutes. No cooking. Serves 4 to 6.

2 cups boiled red kidney beans (rajma)
1 chopped tomato
1 onion, thinly sliced
1 chopped spring onion

To be mixed into a dressing (in a bottle)
3 tablespoons salad oil
1 tablespoon lemon juice
salt and pepper to taste

1.   Mix the beans, tomato, onion and spring onion and arrange in a serving bowl.
2.   Pour the dressing on top and place in the refrigerator.
3.   Just before serving, surround the salad with the shredded lettuce.

Note : You can also make this salad in Indian style by adding 2 tablespoons of chopped coriander, 1 chopped green chilli and 1 teaspoon of lemon juice.

ENSALADA DE GUACAMOLE (GUACAMOLE SALAD)

◀ *The beans and corn are enriched with a smooth dressing of avocado with tomatoes.*

Preparation time : 10 minutes. Cooking time : 10 minutes. Serves 4.

For the vegetables
1 cup boiled red kidney beans (rajma)
2 cups cooked sweet corn kernels
1 cup spring onions, chopped
1 cup lettuce leaves, shredded

To be blended into a dressing (in a bottle)
1 ripe avocado, peeled and cut into pieces
1 tomato, chopped
1 tablespoon vinegar
1 tablespoon oil
$1/4$ teaspoon salt

Pour the dressing over the vegetables and mix well.

Serve cold.

MEXICAN BEAN AND CHEESE SALAD

◀ *A cold salad, comprising of beans, corn and cheese.*

Preparation time : 15 minutes. Cooking time : 10 minutes. Serves 4.

1 cup boiled white beans (chawla)
1 cup boiled red kidney beans (rajma)
1 cup cooked sweet corn kernels
1 cup chopped tomato
$\frac{1}{2}$ cup processed cheese, cut into cubes
1 cup chopped spring onions
2 tablespoons chopped coriander
salt to taste

To be mixed into a dressing (in a bottle)
4 tablespoons salad oil
2 tablespoons lemon juice
$\frac{1}{2}$ teaspoon salt
2 pinches sugar
$\frac{1}{4}$ teaspoon chilli powder

For the topping
chopped spring onions
corn chips, page 26

1. Mix the beans, corn, tomato, cheese, coriander and salt.
2. Add the dressing and onions, mix well and put in a refrigerator to cool.
3. Just before serving, remove from the refrigerator. Add the spring onions and top with corn chips.

Serve cold.

BURNT CORN SALAD

picture on page 18

◀ *Mexicans love their food smoky flavoured. This corn salad is a tasty example.*

Preparation time : 10 minutes. Cooking time : 10 minutes. Serves 4.

$1\frac{1}{2}$ cups cooked sweet corn kernels
1 white onion, sliced
1 capsicum, sliced
1 tomato, sliced
3 teaspoons oil
salt to taste

To be mixed into a dressing (in a bottle)
2 tablespoons olive oil or salad oil
1 tablespoon lime juice
2 pinches chilli powder
a pinch sugar

1   Heat 2 teaspoons of oil in a pan until it smokes.

2.   Add the corn kernels and go on stirring until they are slightly burnt. Remove.

3.   Add the remaining oil and the onion and capsicum and cook for 1 minute. Remove.

4.   Mix the corn kernels, onion, capsicum and tomato and salt.

5.   Pour the dressing on top.

Serve immediately.

FRUIT SALAD WITH BASIL DRESSING

◀ *You can use any combination of fresh fruit with the basil dressing.*

Preparation time : a few minutes. No cooking.

mango slices with melon slices
 or
pineapple slices with watermelon slices
lettuce leaves

For the basil dressing ·
1 cup sour cream, page 77
8 to 10 fresh basil leaves
$^1/_2$ teaspoon sugar
$^1/_4$ teaspoon salt

For the basil dressing
1.   Blend the sour cream with the basil leaves, sugar and salt in a blender.
2.   If you don't get basil leaves, take 2 tablespoons of capsicum pieces, put in boiling water for a few minutes and then blend with sour cream in a blender.

How to proceed
1.   Prepare the fruit and chill.

2.   Before serving, put the fruit in the centre of a salad bowl and surround with lettuce leaves.

3.   Top with the basil dressing.

SALSA

◀ *Use this as a dip or as a sauce with other vegetables.*

Preparation time : 15 minutes. Cooking time : 5 minutes. Makes 1 cup.

3 tomatoes
2 teaspoons chillies in vinegar
1 small onion, finely chopped
1/2 teaspoon chilli powder
1 capsicum
1/4 teaspoon oregano
1/2 teaspoon sugar
1/2 teaspoon salt
1 tablespoon oil

1. Put the tomatoes in hot water for about 10 minutes. Remove the skin and chop.

2. Pierce the capsicum with a fork and hold over the flame until the skin blackens. Remove from the heat, rub off the burnt skin and chop.

3. Heat the oil and fry the onion for 1/2 minute. Add the remaining ingredients and cook for 3 to 4 minutes.

GUACAMOLE

picture on page 35

◀ *Even someone who is indifferent to avocado in other forms is likely to become an avid guacamole fan. To make this Mexican favourite, you mash avocados and then mix them with a choice of seasonings to serve as a dip with chips. You can also use it as a sauce for main dishes, as a dressing for salads or as a filling for tortillas.*

Preparation time : 10 minutes. No cooking. Makes 1 cup.

2 ripe avocados
juice of $1/2$ lemon
1 onion, chopped
1 tomato, chopped
1 green chilli, chopped
salt to taste

1. Cut the avocados in halves. Remove the centres and mash with a fork.

2. Add the lemon juice to prevent darkening and then mix in the remaining ingredients and mash with the back of a fork.

Serve cold as a dip with crackers, corn chips, vegetables etc.

CORN CHIPS WITH SALSA

picture on page 35

◀ *An ever popular Mexican starter.*

Preparation time : 10 minutes. Cooking time : 10 minutes. Serves 4.

For the dough
$1^1/2$ cups finely ground maize flour (makai ka atta)
1 cup plain flour (maida)
4 teaspoons oil
$1/2$ teaspoon ajwain (optional)
$1/2$ teaspoon cumin seeds
salt to taste

Other ingredients
oil for deep frying

For serving
salsa, page 25

1. Roast the cumin seeds on a tava (griddle) for a few seconds. Add the ajwain and roast both again for a few seconds. Pound them coarsely.
2. Mix all the ingredients together and make a dough by adding warm water. Knead very well.
3. Divide the dough into small portions. Roll out each portion thinly with the help of a little flour and prick all over with a fork. Cook lightly on a tava (griddle).
4. Repeat with the rest of the dough.
5. Cut into small squares and deep fry in oil until crisp.
6. Drain thoroughly on absorbent paper. Store in an airtight tin.

Serve with salsa.

NACHOS

◀ *Cheese is melted over corn chips and heated quickly in the oven to make nachos. Guests pull out individual chips to eat with their fingers.*

Preparation time : 10 minutes. Cooking time : 10 minutes. Serves 6.

3 to 4 cups corn chips, page 26
1 cup cooking cheese, grated
2 tablespoons milk
sliced pickle jalapenos, page 77

1. Mix the cheese, milk and 1 tablespoon of water and cook on a slow flame until the cheese melts.
2. Arrange the corn chips on a plate and spread the melted cheese on top.
3. Spread a few pickle jalapenos on top. Grill for a few minutes until the cheese bubbles.

Serve hot.

QUESADILLAS

◀ *Mexican cooks have lots of ways of stuffing a tortilla. This quick and easy one resembles a cheese paratha. A good melting cheese is basic to all fillings of quesadillas. Any other fillings are at the discretion of the cook.*

Preparation time : 20 minutes. Cooking time : 30 minutes. Makes 12 quesadillas.

12 flour tortillas, page 75

To be mixed into a stuffing
100 grams grated cottage cheese (paneer)
50 grams grated cooking cheese
1 green chilli, chopped
1 tomato without the pulp
2 tablespoons cooked corn
salt to taste

Other ingredients
oil for cooking

1.   When you want to serve, spread a little stuffing on one tortilla. Put another tortilla on top and press well so that they stick. Cook on a tava (griddle) spreading a little oil on both sides. Cook until crisp.

2.   Cut into pieces and serve hot.

CHILLI CHEESY ROLL

◄ *An ideal accompaniment with soups.*

Preparation time : 5 minutes. Cooking time : 5 minutes. Makes 1 roll.

1 loaf French bread
butter for the French bread
3 Kashmiri chillies
1 cup grated cooking cheese
2 tablespoons milk

1. Soak the chillies in water. After $^{1}/_{2}$ hour, take out the seeds and chop the chillies.

2. Mix the cheese, milk and 1 tablespoon of water and cook on a slow flame until the cheese melts. Add the chopped chillies to the mixture.

3. Cut the French bread diagonally, apply a little butter and spread the cheese mixture on top. Bake in a hot oven at 200 °C (400° F) for 5 minutes.

Serve hot.

TOMATO CHEESE ROLL

◄ *An ideal starter for the cheese lovers.*

Preparation time : 5 minutes. Cooking time : 5 minutes. Makes 1 roll.

1 loaf French bread
butter for the French bread
1 cup grated cooking cheese
2 tablespoons milk
tomatoes, sliced

1. Cut the French bread diagonally and apply butter lightly to the bread.

2. Mix the cheese, milk and 1 tablespoon of water and cook on a slow flame until the cheese melts.

3. Arrange the tomato slices on the bread and top with the cheese mixture. Bake in a hot oven at 200°C (400°F) for 5 minutes.

Serve hot.

CRUSTY POTATO FINGERS

◀ *An ideal cocktail snack.*

Preparation time : 15 minutes. Cooking time : 15 minutes. Serves 4.

2 potatoes, cut in fingers
finely crushed cornflakes or toasted bread crumbs (for coating)
oil for deep frying

For the batter
1 cup plain flour (maida)
1 tablespoon cornflour
salt to taste

To be made into a paste (for the batter)
1 onion, chopped
2 green chillies, chopped
1/2" (12 mm.) piece ginger
salt to taste

For serving
salsa, page 25

1. Parboil the potatoes in salted water. Drain.

2. Make a batter by mixing the plain flour, cornflour and salt, adding the paste and enough water to make a thick batter.

3. Dip the potato fingers in the batter, roll out in the finely crushed corn flakes or toasted dry bread crumbs and deep fry in hot oil.

Serve hot with salsa.

CRISPY FRIED CAULIFLOWER

◀ *Another good cocktail snack.*

Preparation time : 15 minutes. Cooking time : 15 minutes. Serves 4.

12 large cauliflower florets
finely crushed vermicelli or toasted bread crumbs (for coating)
oil for deep frying

For the batter
1 cup plain flour (maida)
1 tablespoon cornflour
salt to taste

To be made into a paste (for the batter)
1 onion, chopped
2 green chillies, chopped
$1/2$" (12 mm.) piece ginger
salt to taste

For serving
salsa, page 25

1. Parboil the cauliflower florets in salted water. Drain.
2. Make a batter by mixing the plain flour, cornflour and salt, adding the paste and enough water to make a thick batter.
3. Dip the cauliflower florets in the batter, roll out in the finely crushed vermicelli or toasted dry bread crumbs and deep fry in hot oil.

Serve hot with salsa.

CRISPY COTTAGE CHEESE TORTILLAS

◀ *A great starter.*

Preparation time : 10 minutes. Cooking time : 10 minutes. Serves 6.

corn tortilla dough, page 75
oil for deep frying

For the stuffing
200 grams cottage cheese (paneer), cut into small cubes
2 chopped tomatoes
1 chopped onion
1 green chilli, chopped
$1/4$ teaspoon oregano or thyme
2 tablespoons oil
salt to taste

For the topping
fried capsicum strips

1. Roll out the tortilla dough into very small thin rounds.
2. Prick with a fork and deep fry until crisp. Store in an airtight container.

For the stuffing
1. Heat the oil and fry the onion for $1/2$ minute.
2. Add the green chilli and tomatoes and fry again for $1/2$ minute.
3. Add the cottage cheese, oregano and salt and mix well.

How to proceed
1. Put some stuffing on each tortilla round and top with capsicum strips in a cross structure.
2. Repeat with the remaining tortillas and stuffing.

Serve hot.

ASPARAGUS, CHEESE AND CHILLI QUESADILLAS

◀ *Asparagus and cheese make a great filling for quesadillas.*

Preparation time : 10 minutes. Cooking time : 10 minutes. Serves 3.

6 flour tortillas, page 75

For the filling
4 tablespoons chopped asparagus
4 tablespoons grated cooking cheese
1 green chilli, chopped
salt to taste

1. Divide the filling into three parts.
2. Take a tortilla, put $1/_3$rd of the filling on it and press another tortilla on top. Repeat for the remaining tortillas and fillings.
3. Cook on a tava (griddle) on both sides until the cheese melts.
4. Cut each tortilla into four pieces.

Serve hot.

MEXICAN TARTS

picture on page 54

◀ *Mixed vegetables and refried beans topped with sour cream, crushed corn chips and tomato sauce, make a tasty filling for the tarts.*

Preparation time : 15 minutes. Cooking time : 10 minutes. Makes 25 tarts.

Mexican tomato sauce, page 80
3 cups mixed boiled vegetables (corn, potatoes, french beans, carrots)
refried beans, page 74
$1/_2$ cup cottage cheese (paneer)
1 onion, chopped
2 tablespoons oil
salt to taste

For the tarts
1 cup wheat flour (gehun ka atta)
2 cups plain flour (maida)
4 teaspoons oil
$1/_2$ teaspoon salt
oil for deep frying

For the topping
sour cream, page 77
corn chips, page 26, crushed
green onions, chopped
chopped coriander
crispy lettuce leaves ·

Clockwise from top : Coconut and Papaya Drink, page 7; Corn Chips with Salsa, ▶
page 26; Black Bean Soup, page 16; Guacamole, page 25.

For the tarts

1.   Mix the flours, oil and salt and make a semi-stiff dough by adding water.

2.   Knead the dough well and keep for 30 minutes.

3.   Roll out into small puris and press inside a tart mould. Put another puri in another tart mould. Like that build up the layers of puris and tart moulds.

4.   Deep fry the stack in hot oil until crisp.

How to proceed

1.   Heat the oil and fry the onion for 1 minute.

2.   Add the Mexican tomato sauce, vegetables and salt and cook for a few minutes.

How to serve

In each tart, put some vegetable mixture, refried beans and cottage cheese and top with sour cream, crushed corn chips, green onions, coriander and lettuce leaves.

◀ Clockwise from top : Corn on the Cob, page 58; Baked Stuffed Potato Skins, page 48; Mexican Kebabs, page 39; Stuffed Capsicums, page 50.

MOYETTES

picture on page 54

◀ *While these buns seem like lunch fare, they are very popular for breakfast in Mexico. You can make mini Moyettes for a cocktail party. Buy very tasty bread buns or make them at home.*

Preparation time : 15 minutes. Cooking time : 15 minutes. Serves 6.

6 bread buns
6 tablespoons grated cheese
refried beans, page 74
a little butter

For the topping
cabbage, shredded
carrots, grated
1 chopped spring onion
salsa, page 25

1. Cut off the tops from the buns. Scoop out the centres.

2. Fill the centres with some refried beans.

3. Top with some grated cheese and bake in a hot oven at 200 °C (400 °F) for 10 minutes.

4. Take out from the oven and top with the vegetables and salsa.

5. Apply butter lightly on the top and bake for a few minutes until crisp.

Serve hot covered with the bun tops.

MEXICAN KEBABS

picture on page 36

◀ *Kebabs are a favourite barbecue food almost anywhere. The spice mixture gives the Mexican flavour.*

Preparation time : 10 minutes. Cooking time : 10 minutes. Serves 4.

To be mixed into a marinade
2 teaspoons cocoa powder
2 teaspoons chilli powder
1 tablespoon fresh curds
4 cloves crushed garlic
$1/2$ teaspoon oregano
6 tablespoons oil
salt and pepper to taste

Other ingredients
10 capsicum pieces (green and yellow)
10 baby corn pieces, cut into two
10 cottage cheese (paneer) pieces
10 mushrooms
10 white onions, cut into big pieces

For serving
sour cream, page 77
spring onions, chopped

Put the baby corn and mushrooms in hot water. After a few minutes, remove them.

How to proceed

1. Put the capsicum, baby corn, paneer, mushrooms and white onions in the marinade and allow to marinate for 4 to 5 hours.

2. Arrange one piece each of capsicum, baby corn, paneer, mushroom and white onion on individual skewers.

3. Cook on a hot charcoal sigri in front of the guests.

Serve hot with sour cream and spring onions.

COCONUT CURRY FRIED RICE

◀ *Fried rice blends well with this Mexican style coconut curry.*

Preparation time : 30 minutes. Cooking time : 35 minutes. Serves 4.

For the rice
1$^1/_2$ cups uncooked rice
3 tablespoons oil
salt to taste

For the coconut curry
1 coconut
1 white onion, chopped
2 tomatoes, chopped
2 cups mixed boiled vegetables
   (french beans, corn, carrots, potatoes, cauliflower)
1 tablespoon butter
1 tablespoon plain flour (maida)
6 pasilla chillies, page 77
2 pinches sugar
3 tablespoons oil
salt to taste

For the rice
1. Wash and soak the rice for 30 minutes. Drain.
2. Fry the rice in the oil until light pink in colour.
3. Add 3 cups of water and salt and cook until the rice is cooked.

For the coconut curry
1. Grate the coconut. Add 2 cups of water and blend in a liquidiser. Strain and take out the coconut milk. Keep aside.

2. Heat the oil and fry the onion for $^1/_2$ minute.

3. Add the tomatoes and mixed vegetables and cook for a few minutes.

4. Heat the butter, add the flour and cook for 1 minute.

5. Add the coconut milk gradually, stirring constantly until thick.

6. Add the mixture to the mixed vegetables.

7. Add the chillies, sugar and salt and boil for 2 minutes.

Serve hot with the fried rice.

MEXICAN FRIED RICE

picture on page 63

◀ *Most Mexicans fry the rice before cooking. This leaves each individual grain not sticking to each other. This tomato flavoured rice is often served along with refried beans and is also used as a side dish in most meals.*

Preparation time : 30 minutes. Cooking time : 30 minutes. Serves 6

For the rice
1$^1/_2$ cups uncooked rice
3 tablespoons oil
salt to taste

Other ingredients
2 white onions, sliced
3 cloves garlic, crushed
$^1/_4$ teaspoon turmeric powder
1 capsicum, sliced
1 tomato, chopped
1 cup mixed boiled vegetables (french beans, carrots, green peas)
1 teaspoon chilli powder
6 tablespoons oil
salt to taste

For the rice
1. Wash and soak the rice for 30 minutes. Drain.
2. Fry the rice in the oil until light pink in colour.
3. Add 3 cups of water and salt and cook until the rice is cooked.

How to proceed
1. Heat the oil in a broad vessel and fry the onions until golden brown in colour. Add the garlic and fry for a few seconds. Add the turmeric powder and fry again for a few seconds.
2. Remove the onions and in the same oil, fry the capsicum for 1 minute.
3. Add the tomato, vegetables, chilli powder and salt and cook for 1 minute.
4. Add the fried onions and the cooked rice and mix well.

Serve hot.

CHEESY PEPPER RICE

picture on page 53

◀ *A colourful rice combining cheese, capsicum and spices. White onions are used for their special taste and crunchiness.*

Preparation time : 30 minutes. Cooking time : 30 minutes. Serves 6.

For the rice
1¹/₂ cups uncooked rice
3 tablespoons oil
salt to taste

Other ingredients
1 white onion, thickly sliced
3 tablespoons capsicum strips (green, red and yellow)
6 pasilla chillies, page 77
6 cloves garlic, crushed
2 tablespoons grated processed cheese
2 tablespoons oil

salt to taste

For the rice
1. Wash and soak the rice for 30 minutes. Drain.
2. Fry the rice in the oil until light pink in colour.
3. Add 3 cups of water and salt and cook until the rice is cooked.

How to proceed
1. Roast the chillies on a frying pan for a few seconds. Remove from the frying pan and pound with the garlic.
2. Heat the oil and fry the onion and capsicum lightly for $1/2$ minute.
3. Add the chillies and fry for a few seconds.
4. Add the rice, cheese and salt and mix well.

Serve hot.

HUANCIANA PAPAS (POTATOES WITH COTTAGE CHEESE)

◀ *Potatoes tastes great with this lovely cottage cheese sauce.*

Preparation time : 15 minutes. Cooking time : 20 minutes. Serves 4.

4 boiled potatoes, sliced
3 tablespoons butter
salt and pepper to taste

For the sauce
200 grams fresh cottage cheese (paneer)
2 tablespoons milk
1 chopped green chilli
salt to taste

For the baking
2 tablespoons grated cooking cheese

For the sauce
1. Blend the cottage cheese, milk and 2 tablespoons of water in a blender

until smooth.

2. Add the green chilli and salt.

How to proceed

1. Heat the butter, add the potatoes and cook for a few minutes. Sprinkle salt and pepper on top.

2. Arrange the potatoes in a baking dish, spread the sauce over them and top with the cheese.

3. Cover and bake in a hot oven at 200 °C (400 °F) for 10 minutes.

Serve hot.

FRESH CORN ENCHILADAS

picture on page 63

◀ *The ingredients for enchiladas are tortillas, a sauce, a filling and sometimes a garnish, which are then baked. Two enchiladas usually make an ample serving. Traditionally, the only accompaniments are refried beans and plain hot tortillas.*

Preparation time : 20 minutes. Cooking time : 20 minutes. Serves 6.

6 corn tortillas, page 75
Mexican tomato sauce, page 80
oil for deep frying

To be mixed into a stuffing
1½ cups cooked sweet corn
100 grams grated cottage cheese (paneer)
50 grams grated cooking cheese
1 green chilli, chopped
1 tablespoon chopped coriander
1 tomato without the pulp
salt to taste

For the baking
2 tablespoons grated cooking cheese

For the garnish
fresh cream
lemon juice
spring onions

1. Deep fry the tortillas in oil lightly.

2. Pour $1/3$ rd of the Mexican tomato sauce in the bottom of a baking dish.

3. Fill each tortilla with a little stuffing.

4. Arrange each tortilla seam side down in the sauce, arranging side by side in the baking dish. Moisten the tops of the tortillas evenly with the remaining sauce.

5. Sprinkle the cheese over the enchiladas. Bake in a hot oven at 200 °C (400 °F) for 15 minutes.

How to serve
1. Put a lettuce leaf in the centre of a serving plate. Put one enchilada on top.

2. Spoon a little cream mixed with lemon juice. Surround with spring onions and serve.

3. Repeat for the remaining enchiladas.

Note : Probably the greatest sin in enchilada making is to fry the tortillas so long that they become crisp and to bake the dish so long that the tortillas dry out and get crusty on the edges.

TACOS

◀ *Half moon shaped tacos are probably the most popular Mexican food items in America. The word "taco" means "snack" and is generally referred to as a crisp fried corn tortilla folded in half to form a pocket which is filled with a stuffing, garnish and spicy sauce.*

Preparation time : 35 minutes. Cooking time : 40 minutes. Serves 8 to 10.

For the tacos
$1^1/_2$ cups maize flour (makai ka atta)
$1^1/_2$ cups plain flour (maida)
3 teaspoons oil
$^3/_4$ teaspoon salt
oil for deep frying

For the green sauce
Mexican green sauce, page 79

For the stuffing
refried beans, page 74
3 tomatoes, chopped
3 spring onions, chopped
2 cups shredded lettuce leaves
chopped cabbage (optional)
salt to taste

To be mixed into a red sauce
$^1/_2$ cup tomato ketchup
2 teaspoons chilli sauce

For the tacos
1. Mix the flours. Add the oil and salt and make a soft dough by adding warm water.
2. Roll out thin rounds about 4" (100 mm.) in diameter with the help of a little plain flour. Prick lightly with a fork.
3. Deep fry in hot oil on both sides and then bend into a 'U' shape while hot.
4. Store the tacos in an air-tight tin.

How to serve
1. Make a red sauce by mixing the tomato ketchup and chilli sauce.
2. Mix the chopped tomatoes, spring onions, lettuce leaves, cabbage and salt.
3. In the fold of each taco, fill some refried beans, sprinkle some green and red sauce and fill with the chopped vegetables. Again sprinkle a little red sauce and serve.

Alternatively, serve the tacos, stuffing, sauces and chopped vegetables in separate dishes and let your guests make their own fillings.

VARIATION : CORN AND COTTAGE CHEESE TACOS
picture on page 54

for the tacos, page 46
Mexican green sauce, page 79

For the stuffing
1 onion, chopped
2 cups cooked corn kernels
1 cup cottage cheese (paneer), cut into cubes

red capsicum (optional), chopped
1 tomato, chopped
2 tablespoons chopped coriander
2 tablespoons oil
salt to taste

For the topping
a few pieces jalapenos, page 77 or 2 chopped green chillies
olives
lettuce leaves, shredded

For the stuffing
1. Heat the oil and fry the onion for a few seconds.
2. Add the corn, cottage cheese, capsicum, tomato, coriander and salt and mix very well.

How to proceed
In the fold of each taco, sprinkle some green sauce, add the stuffing and top with jalapenos, olives and lettuce.

BAKED STUFFED POTATO SKINS
picture on page 36

◀ *Mushrooms and corn make a great filling for potato skins.*

Preparation time : 15 minutes. Cooking time : 10 minutes. Serves 4.

4 potatoes
grated cooking cheese for baking
oil for deep frying
salt and pepper to taste

1. Boil the potatoes. Cut them lengthwise and scoop out leaving fairly thick walls.

2. Deep fry the potatoes in hot oil until crisp or light pink in colour.

3. Sprinkle salt and pepper over the potatoes.

MUSHROOM FILLING

For the mushroom filling
4 tablespoons finely chopped mushrooms
1 tablespoon chopped onion
1 teaspoon plain flour (maida)
1 finely chopped green chilli
$1/4$ teaspoon oregano
1 teacup white sauce
2 teaspoons butter
salt to taste

For the mushroom filling
1. Heat the butter and fry the onion for $1/2$ minute.
2. Add the flour and green chilli and fry for a few seconds.
3. Add the mushrooms and oregano and cook for 2 minutes or until soft.
Add salt.
4. Add the white sauce and mix well.

CORN FILLING

For the corn filling
2 cups cooked corn
1 onion, chopped
1 green chilli, chopped
2 tablespoons grated cheese
2 tablespoons milk
2 tablespoons fresh cream
2 teaspoons cornflour
2 tablespoons butter
a few drops Tabasco or Capsico sauce
salt to taste

For the corn filling

1. Heat the butter and fry the onion for ½ minute.
2. Add the green chilli and fry again for a few seconds.
3. Add the corn and cook for a few minutes.
4. Mix the milk, cream and cornflour and add to the corn. Cook again for a few minutes, adding salt.
5. Take off the fire, add the cheese and a few drops of Tabasco or Capsico sauce.

How to proceed

1. Put either the mushrooms or corn filling inside the fried skins.
2. Sprinkle the cheese on top and bake in a hot oven at 200 °C (400 °F) for 5 minutes.

Serve hot.

PIMENTAO CON RECHEIO DE OVO
(STUFFED CAPSICUMS)

picture on page 36

◀ *Capsicums are stuffed with a tasty filling of paneer and white sauce.*

Preparation time : 10 minutes. Cooking time : 10 minutes. Serves 4.

2 capsicums

For the stuffing
100 grams cottage cheese (paneer), grated
2 tablespoons white sauce or fresh cream
1 chopped capsicum
½ chopped green chilli
1 tablespoon chopped coriander
salt to taste

For the topping
2 tablespoons grated cooking cheese

1. Cut the capsicums in half. Put in salted boiling water for 3 to 4 minutes and remove.
2. Fill with the stuffing.
3. Cover with the cooking cheese and bake in a hot oven at 200 °C (400 °F) for 10 minutes.

Serve hot.

SPICY MUSHROOM ENCHILADAS

picture on page 53

◀ *Deep fried tortillas are stuffed with a mushroom filling, topped with Mexican tomato sauce and then baked to form enchiladas.*

Preparation time : 20 minutes. Cooking time : 25 minutes. Makes 6 enchiladas.

6 corn tortillas, page.75
Mexican tomato sauce, page 80
oil for deep frying

For the mushroom filling
200 grams fresh mushrooms, chopped
2 onions, chopped
2 tomatoes, chopped
2 green chillies, chopped
1 tablespoon chopped coriander
$1/2$ teaspoon oregano
2 tablespoons cornflour
1 tablespoon oil
salt to taste

For the baking
3 tablespoons grated cooking cheese

For the mushroom filling

1. Heat the oil and fry the onions, tomatoes, green chillies and coriander for a while. Add the chopped mushrooms and fry for a while. Add the oregano and salt.

2. Sprinkle the cornflour over the mushrooms and cook for 2 to 3 minutes.

How to proceed

1. Deep fry the tortillas in oil for a few seconds or until limp.

2. Fill each fried tortilla with the mushroom filling and roll up.

3. Arrange in a baking dish and pour Mexican tomato sauce down the centre of the tortillas.

4. Sprinkle the cheese on top and bake in a hot oven at 200 °C (400 °F) for 20 minutes.

VARIATION : REFRIED BEAN ENCHILADAS

Instead of the mushroom filling, use the mushroom and cottage cheese mixture from Crepes Mexicana, page 60, along with 1 cup refried beans and follow the same method as for spicy mushroom enchiladas.

CORN AND COTTAGE CHEESE CREPES

◀ *Corn, a typical Mexican ingredient, is used with cottage cheese to make a tasty crepe.*

Preparation time : 20 minutes. Cooking time : 25 minutes. Makes 6 crepes.

6 crepes, page 79
1 cup Mexican green sauce, page 79

Top : Spicy Mushroom Enchiladas, page 51; ▶
Bottom : Cheesy Pepper Rice, page 42.

To be mixed into a corn and cottage cheese filling

1¹/₂ cups cooked corn
100 grams grated cottage cheese (paneer)
50 grams grated cooking cheese
1 green chilli, chopped
1 tomato without the pulp
salt to taste

For the baking
3 tablespoons grated cooking cheese

How to proceed

1. Fill the crepes with the corn and cheese filling and fold each one into a triangle.

2. Arrange in a baking dish and pour the Mexican green sauce over them.

3. Sprinkle the cheese on top and bake in a hot oven at 200 °C (400 °F) for 20 minutes.

Serve hot.

SPINACH CREPES

◀ *Spinach and cottage cheese make a good filling for crepes which are topped with Mexican green sauce.*

Preparation time : 20 minutes. Cooking time : 25 minutes. Makes 6 crepes.

6 crepes, page 79
1 cup Mexican green sauce, page 79

◀ Clockwise from top : Moyettes, page 38; Corn Cottage Cheese Tacos, page 47; Mexican Tarts, page 34.

For the spinach filling
3 cups finely chopped spinach
1 chopped green chilli
100 grams cottage cheese (paneer), crumbled
1 chopped onion
1 tablespoon butter
salt to taste

For the baking
3 tablespoons grated cooking cheese

For the filling
1. Heat the butter and fry the onion for 1 minute.

2. Add the spinach and green chilli and fry again for 2 minutes.

3. Add the cottage cheese and salt.

How to proceed
1. Fill the crepes with the spinach mixture and fold each one into a triangle.

2. Arrange in a baking dish and pour the Mexican green sauce over them.

3. Sprinkle the cheese on top and bake in a hot oven at 200 °C (400 °F) for 20 minutes.

Serve hot.

BROCCOLI CREPES WITH MEXICAN GREEN SAUCE

◀ *This recipe is an example of how native Mexican ingredients are adapted to French pancakes. Broccoli and Mexican green sauce make a very tasty combination.*

Preparation time : 20 minutes. Cooking time : 30 minutes. Makes 6 crepes.

6 crepes, page 79
1 cup Mexican green sauce, page 79

For the broccoli filling
$1\frac{1}{2}$ cups broccoli florets, finely chopped
1 onion, chopped
1 green chilli, chopped
4 tablespoons grated cooking cheese
1 tablespoon butter
salt to taste

For the baking
3 tablespoons grated cooking cheese

For the broccoli filling
1.   Put plenty of salted water to boil. When it starts boiling, add the broccoli florets, switch off the gas, cover and leave for 5 minutes. Drain the broccoli.
2.   Heat the butter and fry the onion for $\frac{1}{2}$ minute. Add the green chilli and the broccoli and fry again for 1 minute. Add very little salt.
3.   Cool and add the cheese. Mix well.

How to proceed
1.   Fill the crepes with the broccoli mixture and fold each one into a triangle.
2.   Arrange in a baking dish and pour the Mexican green sauce over them.
3.   Sprinkle the cheese on top and bake in a hot oven at 200 °C (400 °F) for 20 minutes.
Serve hot.

MEXICAN BEAN FAHEETA

◀ *A faheeta is a tortilla stuffed with a bean filling mixed with a variety of salsas and then grilled with cheese.*

Preparation time : 30 minutes. Cooking time : 10 minutes. Makes 12 pieces.

12 flour tortillas, page 75
refried beans, page 74
tomato salsa, page 75
guacamole, page 25
green salsa, page 76
grated cooking cheese

1. Spread a little tomato salsa and guacamole or green salsa on each tortilla.
2. Place some bean filling, fold from both the sides and top with some tomato salsa and cheese.
3. Grill for a few minutes until the cheese melts.

Serve hot.

CORN ON THE COB
picture on page 36

◀ *A good corn on the cob tastes best only with American sweet corn which is yellow. Try eating the kernels raw - yet they taste good. If Indian white corn is used, boil for 25 to 30 minutes and apply salt, pepper, chilli powder and lime juice if desired before serving.*

Preparation time : 5 minutes. Cooking time : 15 minutes. Makes 6 cobs.

6 nos. sweet corn cobs
2 tablespoons butter

1. Clean the corn and trim the stems.
2. Drop the corn in boiling salted water and boil for 10 to 15 minutes.
3. Cover in foil to preserve the heat.

Serve hot with butter.

MEXICAN CHEESE FAHEETA

◀ *This faheeta is for the cheese lovers.*

Preparation time : 30 minutes. Cooking time : 15 minutes. Serves 12.

12 flour tortillas, page 75
tomato salsa , page 75
guacamole, page 25
green salsa, page 76
grated cooking cheese

For the cheese filling
1 cup cottage cheese (paneer), cut into cubes
1 onion, chopped
1 capsicum, chopped
1 small tomato, chopped
1 green chilli, finely chopped
2 tablespoons oil
salt to taste

For the cheese filling
1. Heat the oil and fry the onion and green chilli for 2 minutes.
2. Add the remaining ingredients and cook for a few minutes.

How to proceed
1. Spread a little tomato salsa and avocado salsa on each tortilla.
2. Place some cheese filling, fold from both the sides and top with some tomato salsa, green salsa and cheese.
3. Grill for a few minutes until the cheese melts.

Serve hot.

CHARCOAL ROAST CORN

Preparation time : 5 minutes. Cooking time : 15 minutes. Serves 2.

2 sweet corn cobs
2 tablespoons butter·
lettuce leaves

1. Clean the corn and trim the edges.
2. Brush each corn cob with butter and place in wet lettuce leaves.
3. Seal the corn cob in aluminium foil and put on a charcoal grill, turning it continuously. Cook for 10 to 15 minutes.

Serve hot.

CREPES MEXICANA

◀ *Crepes filled with refried beans and topped with mushrooms, cottage cheese and salsa.*

Preparation time : 20 minutes. Cooking time : 15 minutes. Serves 6.

6 crepes, page 79
1 cup refried beans, page 74

For the mushroom and cottage cheese mixture
2 cups cottage cheese (paneer), cut into cubes
1 onion, chopped
4 tablespoons fresh mushrooms, sliced
2 tablespoons salsa, page 25
1 tablespoon chopped coriander
1/4 teaspoon oregano
2 tablespoons oil

salt to taste

For baking
1 tablespoon milk
3 tablespoons grated cheese

For serving
spring onions
lettuce leaves

1. Heat the oil and fry the onion for 1 minute.

2. Add the mushrooms and fry again for 1 minute.

3. Add the cottage cheese, salsa, coriander, oregano and salt and fry again for a while.

How to proceed
1. In each crepe, first spread some refried beans, then spread some mushroom and cottage cheese mixture.

2. Fold and arrange in a baking dish.

3. Repeat with the remaining crepes.

4. Finally, brush with the milk and top with the cheese.

5. Bake in a hot oven at 200 °C (400 °F) until the cheese melts.

6. Surround with spring onions and lettuce leaves.

Serve immediately with Mexican rice and guacamole.

TOSTADAS

◀ *A whole crisp fried tortilla makes the bottom layer on top of which beans and cheese are piled high. The ingredients traditionally offer contrasts of soft and crisp, hot and cold, sharp and mild. While the Mexicans put meat in their tostadas, this recipe uses cottage cheese.*

Preparation time : 20 minutes. Cooking time : 20 minutes. Serves 6.

6 corn tortillas, page 75
refried beans, page 74
grated processed cheese
shredded iceberg lettuce
sliced tomatoes
avocado slices (optional)
white onion rings
sour cream, page 77
chopped spring onions
oil for deep frying

For the cottage cheese mixture
2 cups cottage cheese (paneer), cut into cubes
1 white onion, chopped
1 tomato, chopped
1 green chilli, finely chopped
1 tablespoon chopped coriander
2 tablespoons oil
salt to taste

For the cottage cheese mixture

1. Heat the oil and fry the onion for $^1/_2$ minute.

2. Add the chopped tomato, green chilli and coriander and fry again for a while.

3. Add the cottage cheese and salt.

Top : Fried Ice-cream, page 71; Bottom : Mexican Fried Rice, page 41 & Fresh Corn Enchiladas, page 44. ▶

How to proceed

1. Deep fry the corn tortillas in oil.
2. On each tortilla, spread some hot refried beans, sprinkle some processed cheese, cover with some cottage cheese mixture, top with shredded lettuce, garnish with a few slices of tomatoes and avocado, some onion rings, a spoon of sour cream and a sprinkling of spring onions.

Serve immediately.

CHIMICHANGAS

◀ *Deep fried burritos with a filling of refried beans, lettuce, cottage cheese accompanied with sour cream and guacamole. Mexicans eat chimichangas just like Indians eat samosas.*

Preparation time : 15 minutes. Cooking time : 15 minutes. Serves 6.

6 flour tortillas (9" i.e. 225 mm. diameter), page 75
refried beans, page 74
oil for deep frying

To be mixed into a filling
6 lettuce leaves, shredded
6 green onions, chopped
2 tomatoes, chopped
100 grams cottage cheese (paneer), chopped
1 green chilli, chopped
salt to taste

◀ Top : Caramel Milk Dessert, page 69;
   Bottom : Eggless Chocolate Mousse, page 72.

Accompaniments
sour cream, page 77
guacamole, page 25
chopped tomatoes

1.   Heat the refried beans and spoon about 2 tablespoons onto the centre of each tortilla.
2.   Spoon about 2 tablespoons of the filling mixture over the beans in the tortilla.
3.   Fold in the sides to make a parcel, making sure that all the filling is enclosed.
4.   Repeat for the remaining tortillas, beans and filling.
5.   Heat oil in a large frying pan and when hot, put the chimichangas, folded side down first. Cook on both sides until crisp. Drain on absorbent paper.
6.   Spoon guacamole over the top of each chimichanga and drizzle sour cream on it. Sprinkle chopped tomatoes on top and serve immediately.

BURRITOS

◀ *Burritos are warm, soft flour tortillas filled with savoury ingredients like beans, cheese, tomatoes and green onions Assemble the fillings and toppings, then let your guest stuff their tortillas with any combination they desire. Top with guacamole and sour cream.*

Preparation time : 10 minutes. No cooking. Serves 6.

6 flour tortillas, page 75

For the filling
refried beans, page 74
grated processed cheese

For the topping
chopped tomatoes
chopped spring onions
guacamole, page 25
sour cream, page 77

1. Place the refried beans, cheese, guacamole, sour cream, tomatoes and spring onions in individual bowls.

2. Let guests make their own burritos by placing the beans and cheese on the tortillas, then applying a spoonful of guacamole and sour cream and topping with chopped tomatoes and spring onions and finally rolling up the tortillas.

BROCCOLI, CORN & JALAPENOS

◀ *Broccoli and corn make a great dish.*

Preparation time : 10 minutes. Cooking time : 10 minutes. Serves 6.

4 cups broccoli, cut into florets
2 cups cooked corn kernels
1 onion, chopped
2 tablespoons sliced and fried almonds
1 tablespoon jalapenos, page 77
2 tablespoons butter
salt to taste

1. Blanch the broccoli in boiling salted water for 3 minutes. Drain.

2. Heat the butter and fry the onion for $1/2$ minute.

3. Add the almonds and fry again until they become crisp.

4. Add the broccoli, corn, jalapenos and salt and fry again for a few minutes.

Serve hot.

TEX MEX PIZZA

◀ *Using flour tortilla as a base, top with beans, corn and cheese and then grill to make this tasty pizza.*

Preparation time : 10 minutes. Cooking time : 10 minutes. Makes 6 pizzas.

12 flour tortillas, page 75
refried beans, page 74
cooked corn kernels
jalapenos
spring onion, chopped
tomato slices

For the topping
12 tablespoons grated cooking cheese
crushed red pepper, page 78

1. Cook the tortillas on a tava (griddle) on moderate heat until crisp.

2. On top of a tortilla, spread some beans, corn, jalapenos, spring onion and tomato slices. Put another tortilla on top. Cover with 2 tablespoons of the cheese and put below the grill until the cheese melts.

3. Repeat with the remaining tortillas and stuffing.

4. Top with crushed red pepper.

Serve hot.

CARAMEL MILK DESSERT

picture on page 64

◀ *The Mexicans love caramel. Here is an excellent milk pudding with a caramel taste.*

Preparation time : 15 minutes. Cooking time : 45 minutes. Serves 6.

2 tablespoons raisins
1 tin (400 gms) condensed milk
500 ml. milk
$1/4$ teaspoon cinnamon powder
$1/2$ teaspoon baking powder
1 cup brown sugar

For decoration
sliced almonds
fresh cream

1. Soak the raisins in warm water (or in rum) for 1 hour.

2. Combine the condensed milk, milk, cinnamon and baking powder. Bring to a boil on a high flame, stirring constantly. Take off the gas.

3. Mix the sugar and $1/4$ cup of water in a saucepan. Bring to a boil, stirring constantly until the sugar dissolves. Pour in the hot milk mixture and mix well.

4. Cook over medium heat, stirring occasionally until the pudding is slightly thick and amber coloured.

5. Add the soaked raisins and refrigerate until well chilled. Just before serving, decorate with almonds and fresh cream.

ICE-CREAM WITH MUSCOVADO SUGAR SYRUP

◄ *Vanilla ice-cream served with cinnamon flavoured sugar syrup.*

Preparation time : 5 minutes. Cooking time : 10 minutes. Serves 4.

4 scoops vanilla ice-cream

For the muscovado sugar syrup
200 grams brown sugar
3" (75 mm.) stick cinnamon
juice of 1 orange
$^1/_4$ teaspoon aniseeds

1. Mix the ingredients for the syrup in a saucepan along with $^1/_2$ cup of water and bring to a boil, stirring occasionally.

2. Simmer over medium heat for 5 minutes.

3. Pour the syrup over the ice-cream and serve immediately.

FRIED ICE-CREAM

picture on page 63

◀ *A favourite Mexican dessert.*

Preparation time : 10 minutes. Cooking time : 1 minute.

a few scoops of vanilla ice-cream
oil for frying

For the batter
1 cup plain flour (maida)

For rolling
crushed corn flakes or desiccated coconut

For the batter
Mix the flour with $1\frac{1}{2}$ cups of water.

How to proceed
1. Chill the ice-cream scoops in the freezer.

2. Dip the ice-cream scoops in the batter and roll into the corn flakes.

3. Deep fry in oil for a few seconds.

Serve with the sauce of your choice.

EGGLESS CHOCOLATE MOUSSE

picture on page 64

◀ *The beauty of this pudding is that it is made without using gelatine.*

Preparation time : 30 minutes. Cooking time : 15 minutes. Serves 6.

2½ cups milk
10 teaspoons sugar
3 teaspoons cocoa powder
100 grams dark chocolate
10 teaspoons china grass (5 grams), cut into small pieces
2 teaspoons custard power
200 grams fresh cream
2 tablespoons powdered sugar
1 teaspoon vanilla essence

1.   Soak the china grass in ³/₄ cup of cold water for 1 hour. Put to cook on a slow flame until it dissolves.

2.   Put 2 cups of milk to boil with the sugar, cocoa powder and dark chocolate.

3.   To the balance ½ cup milk, add the custard powder and boil. When the milk starts boiling, add to the cocoa mixture and go on stirring and cooking for 1 minute.

4.   When the china grass is dissolved completely, add to the boiling custard and cook again for 2 minutes. Strain the mixture and go on stirring it until it is slightly cold.

5.   Beat the cream with the powdered sugar, add the vanilla essence and mix well. Add to the cocoa mixture and put it to set.

6.   Once it sets, chill thoroughly, decorate with cream and chocolate curls and serve cold.

CARAMEL CUSTARD

◀ *Mexicans love the caramelised taste of this light and tasty pudding.*

Preparation time : 60 minutes. Cooking time : 10 minutes. Serves 6.

3 cups milk
3 level teaspoons custard powder
11 teaspoons sugar
$^1/_2$ teaspoon vanilla essence
10 teaspoons china grass (5 grams), cut into small pieces
sugar for caramelising

1. Soak the china grass in $^3/_4$ cup of cold water for 1 hour. Put to cook on a slow flame until it dissolves.

2. In a pudding mould, add the sugar for caramelising and 1 teaspoon of water and go on cooking until it becomes brown. Spread it all over the mould, rotating the mould to spread the sugar evenly. The sugar will harden in 10 minutes.

3. Keep aside $^1/_2$ cup milk. Mix the custard in this cold milk.

4. Boil the remaining milk with the sugar. When the milk starts boiling, add the custard and go on cooking until you get a smooth sauce.

5. Add the china grass to the custard. Boil again for 2 minutes. Strain the mixture and cool it slightly.

6. Add the vanilla essence. Mix well. Pour this mixture over the prepared mould. Put it to set.

7. Before serving, loosen the sides with a sharp knife and invert on a plate.

REFRIED BEANS

◀ *Mexico's famous 'refried beans' aren't really refried at all. 'Re' in Spanish means 'very' or 'thoroughly'. This famous dish appears on Mexican tables at every meal from breakfast to midnight snacks, as beans are economical, delicious and nutritious. They keep well when refrigerated.*

Preparation time : 15 minutes. Cooking time : 15 minutes. Makes 4 cups.

$1^1/_2$ cups red kidney beans (rajma)
2 large tomatoes, chopped
1 clove garlic, crushed
2 to 3 green chillies, finely chopped
2 large onions, chopped
$^1/_2$ teaspoon chilli powder
1 teaspoon roasted cumin seed powder
2 teaspoons sugar
2 tablespoons butter
2 tablespoons oil
salt to taste

1. Wash the beans and soak in water overnight. Next day, drain.

2. Add the tomatoes, garlic, green chillies and half the onions and put to cook in a pressure cooker. Drain. Keep aside the drained water.

3. Heat the oil and fry the remaining onions for $^1/_2$ minute.

4. Add the beans, chilli powder, cumin seed powder, sugar, butter and salt and cook for 2 to 3 minutes.

5. Mash the beans coarsely.

6. If the mixture is dry, add the drained water.

Serve hot.

FLOUR TORTILLAS

◀ *With the Spanish influence, wheat flour was introduced in Mexico and was quickly used for making tortillas. However, flour tortillas are not that extensively used in Mexican cooking.*

Preparation time : 15 minutes. Cooking time : 5 minutes. Makes 12 tortillas.

1 teacup wheat flour (gehun ka atta)
2 teacups plain flour (maida)
4 teaspoons oil
$1/2$ teaspoon salt

1. Mix the flours, oil and salt and make a dough by adding enough warm water.

2. Knead the dough well and keep for $1/2$ hour. Knead again.

3. Depending on the diameter you require for the dish, roll out the dough into 6" (150 mm.) or 9" (225 mm.) diameter thin rounds with the help of a little flour.

4. Cook lightly on a tava (griddle) and keep aside.

Tip : Make large quantities and freeze in a refrigerator, as tortillas are used extensively in Mexican food. They should be present at every Mexican meal, served warm, stacked within a warm white cloth, and then placed inside a colourful straw basket.

CORN TORTILLAS

◀ *Tortillas are the bread of Mexico, being flat, round and unleavened. They can be stacked, rolled, folded, torn, cut and crumbled. They taste good whether eaten soft and hot, crisp fried or toasted.*

Preparation time : 15 minutes. Cooking time : 5 minutes. Makes 12 tortillas.

1¹/₂ teacups maize flour (makai ka atta)
1 teacup plain flour (maida)
3 teaspoons oil
³/₄ teaspoon salt

1. Mix the flours, oil and salt and make a dough by adding enough warm water.

2. Knead the dough well and keep for ¹/₂ hour. Knead again.

3. Depending on the diameter you require for the dish, roll out the dough into 6" (150 mm.) or 9" (225 mm.) diameter thin rounds with the help of a little flour.

4. Cook lightly on a tava (griddle) and keep aside.

Tip : Make large quantities and freeze in a refrigerator, as tortillas are used extensively in Mexican food. They should be present at every Mexican Meal, served warm, stacked within a warm white cloth and then placed inside a colourful straw basket.

GREEN SALSA

3 large green tomatoes
1 onion, chopped
4 to 5 green chillies, chopped
2 teaspoons white vinegar (approx.)
salt to taste

1. Cut the tomatoes into big pieces. Add the onion, green chillies and ¹/₂ teacup of water and cook.

2. When cooked, blend in a liquidiser and strain.

3. Add the vinegar and salt.

PICKLE JALAPENOS

250 grams green chillies
50 ml. vinegar
1 tablespoon sugar
1 tablespoon salt

1. Slice the green chillies and discard the seeds.
2. Mix the vinegar, sugar and salt. Add 2 cups of water and boil.
3. Switch off the gas and add the chillies.

Store in a bottle and use when required.

SOUR CREAM

◀ *As sour cream is not available in India, this recipe is suggested as a substitute.*

200 grams fresh cream
1 to 2 tablespoons thick curds
2 pinches salt

1. Beat the cream until thick.
2. Add the curds and salt and mix well.

PASILLA CHILLIES

6 red chillies, fat and thick (Kashmiri or resham patti)

1. Cut the chillies open. Discard the stems and seeds.

2. Cut into small pieces with scissors.

3. Place in a bowl and cover with boiling water. Allow to stand for 45 to 60 minutes.

4. Drain.

SERRANO CHILLIES

green chillies which have turned red in a few days time but are not totally dry.

CRUSHED RED PEPPER

This product is simply a dried hot red pepper which has been crushed. You may have seen it on the table in Italian restaurants.

Pound dry red chillies coarsely.

BROWN STOCK

Preparation time : 15 minutes. Cooking time : 15 minutes. Makes 6 cups.

2 carrots
10 french beans
1 onion
1 potato
2 large tomatoes
a small piece of cabbage or white pumpkin (lauki)

1. Cut all the vegetables into big pieces.

2. Add 6 cups of water and cook in a pressure cooker.

3. When cooked, blend in a blender and pass through a sieve.

MEXICAN GREEN SAUCE (FOR BAKING)

1/2 large capsicum
2 cups milk
2 tablespoons butter
2 tablespoons plain flour (maida)
salt and pepper to taste

1.   Put the capsicum in boiling water. After a few minutes, take out and blend with the milk in a blender.

2.   Heat the butter and fry the flour for 1/2 minute. Add the blended milk and go on stirring until the sauce becomes thick.

3.   Add salt and pepper.

CREPES

◄ *Mexicans have adopted the French crepes, innovating with different stuffings. They are also used in desserts.*

Preparation time : 15 minutes. Cooking time : 25 minutes. Serves 6.

1/2 cup plain flour (maida)
1/2 cup cornflour
1/2 cup milk
2 teaspoons melted butter
a pinch salt

1.   Mix the plain flour, cornflour, milk and salt with 1/2 teacup of water.

2.   Spread 2 tablespoons of the batter onto a non-stick frying pan and cook on both sides with a little butter. Repeat for the remaining batter.

MEXICAN TOMATO SAUCE (FOR BAKING)

1 kg. red tomatoes
1 onion, chopped
1 green chilli, chopped
$1/2$ teaspoon chilli powder
$1/4$ teaspoon oregano
2 pinches sugar
2 tablespoons oil
salt to taste

1. Put the tomatoes in hot water for 10 minutes. Take out the skin and chop them.

2. Heat the oil and fry the onion for $1/2$ minute. Add the green chilli and fry again for a few seconds.

3. Add the tomatoes, chilli powder, oregano, sugar and salt.